Midland

Other Works by Kwame Dawes

Poetry

Progeny of Air
Resisting the Anomie
Prophets
Requiem
Jacko Jacobus
Shook Foil
Mapmaker

Anthologies

Wheel and Come Again: An Anthology of Reggae Poems

Nonfiction

Natural Mysticism: Towards a New Reggae Aesthetic
Talk Yuh Talk: Interviews with English-Speaking Caribbean Poets

Midland

Kwame Dawes

OHIO UNIVERSITY PRESS

ATHENS

Ohio University Press, Athens, Ohio 45701
© 2001 by Kwame Dawes
Printed in the United States of America

Ohio University Press books are printed on acid-free paper ♾ ™

09 08 07 06 05 04 03 02 01   5 4 3 2 1

Library of Congress Cataloging-in-Publication Data

Dawes, Kwame Senu Neville, 1962–
     Midland : poems / by Kwame Dawes.
        p.   cm.
     ISBN 0-8214-1355-4 (alk. paper) — ISBN 0-8214-1356-2 (pbk.: : alk. paper)
        I. Title.

PR9265.9.D39 M5 2000
811'.54—dc21

00-044615

For
Lorna,
Sena, Kekeli, and Akua,
Mama the Great
and the tribe:
Gwyneth, Kojo, Aba, Adjoa, Kojovi

Acknowledgments

Acknowledgments are made to *London Review of Books, Yemassee, Poetry London Newsletter, Ariel, Callaloo, Double Take Magazine, Obsidian II, Poetry Review, Kunapipi, Spoon River Poetry Review, Caribbean Writer, Wasafiri,* and *Renaissance Noire/Black Renaissance*, where some of these poems originally appeared.

"Midland," "Map Maker," "Inheritance," and "Holy Dub" all appeared in *Mapmaker*, a chapbook published by Smith/Doorstop in the U.K. (2000).

Contents

III

IV

I

Inheritance

O Christ, my craft and the long time it is taking!

Derek Walcott

I

In the shade of the sea grape trees the air is tart
with the sweet sour of stewed fruit rotting
about his sandalled feet. His skin,
still Boston pale and preserved with Brahman
devotion by the hawkish woman
who smells cancer in each tropical wind,
is caged in shadows. I know those worn eyes,
their feline gleam, mischief riddled;
his upper lip lined with a thin stripe
of tangerine, the curled up nervousness
of a freshly shaved mustache. He is old
and cared for. He accepts mashed food
though he still has teeth—she insists and love
is about atoning for the guilt
of those goatish years in New England.
A prophet's kind of old. Old like casket-
aged genius. Above, a gull surveys
the island, stitches loops through the sea and sky—
an even horizon, the bias on which
teeters a landscape, this dark loam of tradition
in which seeds split into tender leaves.

II

The smudge of colors spreads and dries in the sun.
The pulpy paper sucks in the watercolor,
and the cliché of sea and a fresh beach
seems too easy for a poem. He has written
them all, imagined the glitter and clatter
of silver cuirasses, accents of crude
Genoese sailors poisoning the air,
the sand feeling for the first time the shadow
of flag and plumed helmet—this old story
of arrival that stirred him as a boy,
looking out over the open plains,
as he cluttered the simple island
with the intrigues of blood and heroes,
his gray eyes searching out an ancestry
beyond the broad laughter and breadfruit-
common grunts of the fishermen, pickled
with rum and the *picong* of *kaiso*,
their histories as shallow as the trace
of soil at the beach's edge where crippled
corn bushes have sprouted. That was years ago;
he has now exhausted the jaundiced language
of a broken civilization.
These days he just chips at his epitaph,
a conceit of twilights turning into
bare and bleak nights. He paints, whistling
Sparrow songs while blistering in the sun.

III

The note pad, though, is not blank. The words start,
thirteen syllables across the page, then seven
before the idea hesitates. These days
he does not need to count, there is in his head
a counter dinging an alarm like the bell
of his old Smith Corona. His line breaks
are tidy dramas of his entrances
and exits, he will howl before the darkness.
This ellipsis is the tease of a thought,
the flirtatious lift of a yellow skirt
showing a brown taut thigh—a song he knows
how to hum but can't recall the lyrics, man—
an airy metaphor—taken up
by a flippant sea breeze going some place
inland, carrying the image, snagged
by the olive dull entanglement
of a thorny patch. At eight he lays
the contents of his canvas book bag
on the sand, organizing the still life
like honed stanzas. He scoops the orange pulp
of papaya, relishing the taste of fruit, this bounty
harvested from the ant-infested fragile tree
that bleeds each time its fruit is plucked.
The flesh is sunny. He knows the fishermen warn
it will cut a man's nature, dry up
his sap; that women feed their men pureed
papaya in tall glasses of rum-punch
to tie them down, beached, benign pirogues
heading nowhere. He dares the toxins
to shrivel him, to punish him

for the chronic genius of crafting poems
from the music of a woman's laugh
while he chews slowly. A poem comes to him
as they sometimes do in the chorus
of a song. It dances about in his head.
He does not move to write it down—it will wait
if it must, and if not, it is probably
an old sliver of long discarded verse.

IV

The old men in the rum shop are comforted
as they watch him limp along the gravel
road, wincing at the sharp prod of stones
in his tender soles, the knees grinding
at each sudden jar—just another ancient
recluse with his easel folded under
his arm, a straw hat, the gull-gray eyes
seeing the sea before he clears the hill.
They know him, proud of the boy—bright as hell
and from good people. There is no shared language
between them, just the babel of rum talk
and cricket sometimes. Under his waters
he talks of Brussels, Florence, barquentines,
Baudelaire, rolling the words around
like a cube of ice—they like to hear
the music he makes with tongue; the way
he tears embracing this green island,
this damned treasure, this shit hole of a treasure.
Sometimes if you don't mind sharp, you would think
him white, too, except for the way him hold
him waters, carry his body against the sun
with the cool, cultivated calm of a rumhead.
Him say home like it come from a book;
hard to recognize when him say home
that is this dry beachhead and tired earth
him talking. They like it, anyway, the way
they like to hear "Waltzing Matilda" sung
with that broad Baptist harmony to a *cuatro*
plunked, to hear it fill an old song night.

V

If he is my father (there is something
of that fraying dignity, and the way
genius is worn casual and urbane—aging
with grace) he has not lost much over the years.
The cigarette still stings his eyes and the scent
of Old Spice distilled in Gordon's Dry Gin
is familiar here by the sea where a jaunty
shanty, the cry of gulls and the squeak
of the rigging of boats are a right backdrop—
but I have abandoned the thought, the search
for my father in this picture. He's not here,
though I still come to the ritual death watch
like a vulture around a crippled beast,
the flies already bold around its liquid
eyes, too resigned to blink. I have come
for the books, the cured language, the names
of this earth that he has invented,
the stories of a town, and the way
he finds women's slippery parts in the smell
and shape of this island, the making
and unmaking of a city through
the epic cataclysm of fire,
eating the brittle old wood, myths dancing
in the thick smoke like the gray ashen debris
of sacrifice. It is all here with him—
this specimen living out his twilight days,
prodigious as John's horror—the green
uncertain in the half light. When we meet
he is distant, he knows I want to draw
him out, peer in for clues. He will not be drawn out,

he is too weary now. He points his chin
to the rum shop, to an old man, Afolabe,
sitting on the edge of a canoe, black
as consuming night. I can tell
that he carries a new legend in his terrible
soul each morning, a high tower over the sea.

VI

I could claim him easily, make of him
a tale of nurture and benign neglect;
he is alive, still speaks, his brain clicks
with the routine of revelations
that can spawn in me the progeny
of his monumental craft. These colonial
old men, fed on cricket and the tortured
indulgences of white schoolmasters
patrolling the mimic island streets
like gods growing gray and sage-like in the heat
and stench of the Third World; they return
to the reactionary nostalgia
during their last days—it is the manner
of aging, we say, but so sad, so sad.
I could adopt him, dream of blood and assume
his legacy of a divided self.
But it would ring false quickly; after all
my father saw the Niger eating out
a continent's beginnings; its rapid
descent to the Atlantic; he tasted
the sweet *kelewele* of an Akan
welcome, and cried at the uncompromising
flame of *akpetechi*. The blood of his sons
was spilled like libation into the soil, and more:
in nineteen twenty-six, an old midwife
buried his bloodied navel string, and the afterbirth
of his arrival, at the foot of an ancient
cotton tree there on the delta islands
of Calabar. My blood defines the character
of my verse. Still, I pilfer (a much better word),

rummage through the poet's things to find the useful,
how he makes a parrot flame a line
or a cicada scream in wind; the names
he gives the bright berries of an island
in the vernacular of Adam and the tribe.

VII

I carry the weight of your shadow always,
while I pick through your things for the concordance
of your invented icons for this archipelago.
Any announcement of your passing
is premature. So to find my own strength,
I seek out your splendid weaknesses.
Your last poems are free of the bombast
of gaudy garments, I can see the knobs
of your knees scarred by the surgeon's incisions
to siphon water and blood from bone;
I stare at your naked torso—the teats
hairy, the hint of a barreled beauty
beneath the folding skin. I turn away
as from a mirror. I am sipping your blood,
tapping the aged sap of your days while you grow
pale. You are painting on the beach, this is how
the poem began—I am watching you watching
the painting take shape. I have stared long enough
that I can predict your next stroke—your dip
into the palette, your grunts, your contemplative
moments, a poised crane waiting for the right
instance to plunge and make crimson ribbons
on a slow moving river. These islands
give delight, sweet water with berries,
the impossible theologies
of reggae, its metaphysics so right
for the inconstant seasons of sun and muscular
storm—you can hear the shape of a landscape
in the groan of the wind against the breadfruit
fronds. I was jealous when at twenty, I found

a slim volume of poems you had written
before you reached sixteen. It has stitched in me
a strange sense of a lie, as if all this
will be revealed to be dust—as if I learned
to pretend one day, and have yet to be found out.

Hoarding

For Sarah Maguire

She is hoarding poems these days, the ideas
anyway; keeping them for a later time
when her language will be distilled to the pine
lacquer of aged metaphors — efficient as ancient
music, the composer at her height. She is
sure of this, that she grows swollen and graceful
in time, her poems sweetly succulent and free
of the gristle of youth. It is a miserly art,
keeping the gems for later. Truth be told,
she returns to old poems with regret, a pained
annoyance at the too rash youth casting
amateurish molds, filled with the bubbles
of inexperience, ideas that in the raw clay
are simply gifted, the stuff of higher verse,
but caught in her too careless craft,
contort grotesquely, failed artifacts.
She has fallen short and will not forgive
youth for such waste. So these days,
in deference to the seventy-year-old,
white-headed slack-breasted dowager poet,
she foregoes the poems, the elegies too delicate
for her meager gifts, still uncertain. She knows
so little now. She makes lists of poems
to be written: a memory of a mango's taste,
the imperial grace of lilacs, the melody
of a Handel hymn, a lament for the beloved dead.

Ska Memory

For Neville Dawes (1926–1984)

The streets of this city are spaces where the body recalls
the saunter of pleasure and fear, where the possession
of the groove, the maddening tattoo is a relentless language.
In this dusty city, sudden as the klaxon calls, the drum
rolls a clatter of a garbage bin and the engine jumps into frenetic
yelps from its belly. We dip and move, while a horn-man tilts his hat,
draws deep and blows a soft hill rising into a mountain, the shape
of his woman's pubis at half light, the echo left by a lost pea-dove,
fading into time, and we know we are traveling into a history
older than these streets, a history kept in a song, smelling
of old sweat, iron of dried blood, the bitter reek of bodies.
Alive now, I count the thirty-six bars, a circle of order
and madness, calculating the genius of a rift that clears
the mountain then faces greenly into the night. Those arias
are thick-lipped and dark like me, they are the old rag
of a bluesman. You told me once to listen to the way
a melody could collect memories, could flesh and swell
and bleed, and though you are long dead, I thank you for it.

Holy Dub

> . . . round
> my mud hut I hear again
> the cry of the lost
> swallows, horizons' halloos, found-
> ationless voices, voyages
>
> *Kamau Brathwaite*

I

Let us gather, then, the legend of faith,
truth of our lives in this crude foment of days.

We are so afraid to look to the sky, so cowed, we whisper
of straight paths while a nation grows fat on its own flesh.

Our gospel—our testament—makes martyrs of us.
Another life,
scribbles the scribe, his parchment sucking the blood
of root dyes.

We keep these hymns we've sung through time as stations of our
    journeys.

Come to the waters
There is a vast supply,
There is a river,
That never shall run dry.
Hallelujah!

II

His afro recedes, creeping towards the nape creaturely,
his forehead is a veined, leathered casing.

The lamplight is guarded by the soot-stained,
wafer-thin glass, with its simple web of doilies

in pale yellow paint—such basic
craft, such splendor in useful things.

He is writing himself into a brittle savannah,
and the mother's calm song he hears is the meaning of faithfulness.

Too-too bobbii
Too-too bobbii.

Her sound carries for miles while her choleric
child fatigues the night with a wailing counterpoint.

The remembrance of old blood makes his skin
accept the sun. The livery is long burnished.

The music of lullabies turns about the poet's head.
His skin has grown darker here—*obroni* black man.

He speaks Ewe, understands the pidgin of mosquitoes.

III

Between click-filled night and pink dawn,
Beethoven's miserable lament

circles the bungalow that squats beneath the naked
mesh of a *yoyi*'s canopy. He finds comfort

in this music, so like the orange dry of the grass lands,
the deep blues of memory. In the symphony's turn

is a thick sweetness of cheap wine and the substance
of fresh bread, still warm, broken by rough hands.

He records the gospel of the desert people,
poor folk whose mornings are oblations to light.

This poet is a *griot* in search of a village. He will forget
all dreams come sunlight. He fears this most.

For decades they will remain myths of a better life,
until he reaches the wilderness of his last dawns,

in a too cold loft over Greenwich Village where he will
try to make verse like they used to make psalms:

to last and last.

Liminal

I should have been born in the epoch of flesh
mongering, the time of moral malaise, to hear
the blues crawling from the steaming dungeons
of first blues folk; their lyric moaning
against the encroaching gloom;
I should have heard the iambic ebb and roll
of sea lapping against an alien shore,
the boom of wind in sails, the quick-repeat
auctioneer's scatology, that maddening knocking.
But I've arrived in this other time, waiting
upon an old woman's prayer, to carry the tears and laughter
so long preserved in the tightly knotted hem
of her skirt where she keeps herbs, a broken tooth,
cowrie shells, kola nuts, and the soft lavender
of a wild flower's petals; aged good and strong.
I am gathering the relics of a broken threnody,
lisping psalms—all I have—and crying salt and wet.

Timehri

After all, it is not about the dialects of this edge
of a bloody century, it is the texture of spirit
caught up in the earth. I am a door if you catch
the earth rhythm of my dream, and this music
is below me, below us all. We are standing on a pliant
floor, while the bass of the song trembles
everything; it is here in this moment that light,
color, and *timehri* whisper.

I arrive at the dusty graves of my ancestors
somewhere in Ewe country looking for names and dates,
hieroglyphs of belonging. There are no names on the stones.
I find my feet trembling as the women's dirge startles
the tambourines; and God is brilliant in the morning sky;
Jesus stirring the dirt, his terrible music swirling.

Memory: An Abstraction

After Shostakovich's Quartet #10, Opus 118 *by Aubrey Williams*

1

At the edge the dusk silhouettes a tree's delta
of branches over a spot of red sky.
In the middle the sun is a smear of bone white.
Yellow streaks of egg yolk and the solid vertebrae,
spotted vermilion with flesh, frame everything.
This image too, uncertain as the music
that traps the seasons in myth,
finds its constant peace in my dreams.

2

The waterfalls thunder while ghosts whisper their ragged
tales, strips of old cloth flitting in the breeze
despite the groan of the storm in the pound of water.
Above, the sky breaks into shadow. We cannot find our way
back for the charts betray us. We rely on the stars,
but cloud cover mutes the night with flat silence.
We cannot travel in the daytime so we shout and listen.
We have stumbled into language, touching the stones
with our bare feet—these cool humped alphabets sprayed
with water beneath a gray unfeeling dawn.

Caricature

Naked, standing at ease, a man
about to be shot at the edge of an ocean,
his body is old, the eyes morose,
the flesh on him is loose.

There is nothing sexual in the dumb
hang of his dark penis, in the clump
of pubic hairs, in the way his thighs,
cellulite and dark patches of scarred skin,
touch. He has a woman's hips.
His hands, when he brings them to his face, seem
small, useless, all too soft, and he looks
ordinary enough to be a condemned man.

This is the face he sees at twelve midnight:
cheeks rounding, eyes tiny, too far buried,
forehead dry, taut, and starting to crack.

He wears white briefs, a T-shirt, a Seiko watch
to bed at night. Sometimes she turns to him,
holds him, sometimes not. He lies here staring
into the black until he sees the weft of coconut
fronds, unfolding above him, and hears the sharp
cracking of rifles above the groan of the ocean and wind.

Sanctuary

From here the village is cradled in the slopes,
smeared into restless rings by a palette knife,
the trees bending into swirls of blackened green-blue
edged with amber like the heads of saints.

A burnt-out cedar rises full,
its jagged steeple pricking the night.
This spill of moonglow makes the zinc in the roofs wave
as if nothing is permanent, nothing but these patterned hills
fading against a play of stars that run paths in loops
while the sickle moon longs to be a sun, all yellow,
spectacularly blurred against my bruised cornea.
With one eye closed, everything mists into a whirl of stars
until I too am looping into its infinite streaks,
forgetting that behind me
you are still weeping,
rehearsing my betrayal.

There is no comfort in the rotted cedar's holiness,
no open door of forgiveness. I feel the moon on my skin.
Somewhere a radio gently carries a melody from another country,
the swooping, nonchalant dance of a love letter in the breeze.

Genocide

After Olmec-Mayan — May Confrontation *by Aubrey Williams*

Across the flame the skulls quarrel.
We listen to them like we listen to wind.

1

The artificial village grows confused when it spills
into the crude haphazard of the centuries-old hovels. The sundial sits

on an open plateau overlooking the village. Here history
is offered for a modest entry fee in Northern Irish currency.

They arrive despite the news of bombs shattering
the scarred muscle of Belfast's heart. I can see the blood

of bare feet rotting in potato-blighted peat. I read time:
the arc of the sun in a knife's shadow. I am reading someone else's myths.

2

The Irish learned quickly to scalp neatly, grateful always for the long
    sable hair
that wrapped thick around bloody fists. Killing turns into habit as
    pragmatic

as the slaughter of prairie dogs spotting God's open fields — the bounty
of suffering and sweat — old as bitter ale, old as the black salty blood of
    lambs.

3

I trace patterns on the rugged cured hide of an old cow.
It is not my culture, but this dialect of genocide,

this forgetting and retrieving with the drum,
this swirl of spirits, this dogged faith

in the whispering of trees, this blurred memory,
this broken village where everything is eaten by hunger

is my birthright. My craft
takes to the flame and color well.

I see no eyes, just the heads, the off-white jaws
going, the rabbit teeth chattering sudden death.

4

The air reeks after rain. The bodies rot.
Naked graves. Bones are tombstones.

The flies hum a sound, a drone of breaths,
last breaths while skin pulps, then falls away.

It is morning and a cow rots where a pasture thrived.
Dandelions glow painterly against a fence.

All flesh turns black.
See the toes?
Black.

Sun Strokes

For Sena

1

My daughter tells me that the sun is a ball of gasses;
that flames are hard to define, but heat she understands:
pressure plus gasses equals heat.
These equations, she explains—she is six this month.

2

Bonfires around martyrs were merciful—why my daughter
knows this is beyond me.

Wet straw stuffed into the dark cleavages in the bramble
before the execution

caused the smoke to kill—a few coughs, then an airless, painless death
while the muttering

priests repeated Hail Mary's full of grace—my daughter tells me
most of this. A prelude

to an impossible question, I fear. But she has no questions,
she just asks, *Did you know?*

3

Sometimes I see a bloated head in the sun,
the shape of a boxer's clean-shaven head from behind.
I am seeing paintings the way my daughter does—
finding the poetics of discovery in the things I don't know.

There, see that swath of red paint—
it is a flame frolicking over his crumbling back,
red patterns sending threads of yellow smoke into the blue,
all dancing at the edges of the sun—the gasses, the heat:

Sunspot Maximum.

At the edges everything flakes into a sun-beaten smear of oil
on uncured canvas, the way art rots in the humid tropics.

4

All that is left is a scream that makes us turn only to be
    blinded by the sun.

Amber threads web our vision's edge with false gold, unreliable
    as the scream we heard.

It was not my daughter, though I thought it was. I imagined it.
    She is sitting there

among open art books, telling stories to herself—a sweet
    calculus of faith.

Map Maker

After Fenwick

. . . As I was saying—is so bush work stay. Especially on a job like this. . . .
Just bide your time. Another couple morning, the survey done, you pack
you bag and home, Canje cobweb left behind.

Wilson Harris

I

In a tinderbox frame, the light leaks
through gaps in the rotting panels
and salt air from the sea and brackish river
softens the collected folders until they green and bleed
into the wood, returning to the roaches,
to the smell of worms, to the earth, to the tick of parasites.

An old man with glassed eyes and skin
like the insides of a tangerine peel, guides me
through the shelves to the dank corner smelling
of jungle funk so thick it lingers like the touch
of dew on the skin long after the sun.

II

He tells me how the novelist made maps in another life.
I tell him that the man is older now and sips tiny cups
of green tea as he stares through the misted panes
of his English cottage, the house smelling too much
of gas and boiling cabbage.

The librarian smiles, his wrinkles showing at last.
He leads me slowly along corridors, then unties the folders
to show me the neat, clean-edged surveyor's charts
of my friend the novelist. His lettering is even as always,
and the circular patterns of the earth's topography
are carefully mapped on the jaundiced sheets.
His notes read like a man reporting discovery for the first time,
with muted awe, yet dutiful to detail like a soldier.

His companions are all listed in the tidy ledger
of laborers, porters, cooks, guides, and poets
(like the drunk who fled from his wife, his daughter,
his nation, and a demon poem that turned septic on him
one too still night of hubris and rum, the man who talked
to his shadow and cursed his ear for the sounds it ate),
their wages, their debts, their rations their vanishings.

III

It is harder, though, to chart the smell of a country,
the concentric mixing of the mud-washed
market with its brown earth-heavy scent
of vegetables bleeding; yams, like elephantine
fingers, white and seeping where the knife
cuts; the impotent regularity of lime green
okras; the glowing violet of obscene garden eggs.
How do you sketch the rotting scent of a mammal's
carcass dangling from rusty hooks, trying
to suck in the salt sea spray to preserve itself
from the crawl of maggots? How do you write
the city's stench, the gutters breeding mosquitoes
as huge as wasps, giddy drunk and brazen like flies?
This earth defies the cartographer's even lines,
the tidy predictability of shapes, the neat names with precise
capitals, no smudge, no uncertainty of the hand. It is hard to tell
that the land has shifted, blooming new contours.
The charts cannot change as fast as the ironic jungle.
We have come this way before, I am certain,
but the landmarks are not exactly what they were.
The river is now a bow, now a crescent where once
it was straight, or so it seemed. The natives ask no questions;
they sniff the air, move their eyes, and live.
The cartographer, I know, understands the fiction
of this telling, the lines are myths, dream-stories
in the faces of his crew. The only constant is the psychotic
lament of Wagner and a bloody warrior wail from the Warrau soldier
who has followed the scent of this march for weeks like a breeze.
The notes of music are caught in the foliage.
On the way back, they have only just begun to drop
like shed leaves in the blackened creeks of this hinterland.

IV

Across the river's mouth, light circles still the slow water into glass
and a canoe silhouettes poetically; the body of its pilot
is a divining twig leaning towards the mawing delta.
Sometimes it seems a joke, this ordering of dreams, this flattening
of the history of the world, of the heart into a faded yellow chart.
And when we least expect it, the jungle bursts through
the thin parchment, splitting it to shreds, leaving us lost again.

The novelist is dying now, and with him a generation of dialects
to speak the earth, the mist, the light, the river. There is no language
on the water, all is cloudy. Soon the canoe is a mere smudge.

Two Premonitions

1

Crossing the Thames

> God only knows,
> God makes his plan
> the information's not available to the mortal man
>
> *Paul Simon*

My friend the writer has not been well. In the face of it
blasé dismissals suggesting that we all
are slowly dying too seem patently trite.
We are crossing the Thames, staring at
the uncommon dignity of London's skyline,
and I imagine him gone. The sudden cavity
slows me to a death walk: I have no tools
to carry me through the moment. I am humbled
by the dignity of his wit, his faith in words.

2

Embroidery

He has sewn with delicate care the clues
of his fading into the fine embroidery
of his immaculate lines. To find the trace of despair
in the elegant élan of white lace, I must

pick at the knotted strings, making thread-
bare the ordered mesh until I find the painful evidence
of his pending flight. I read, instead, the intact patterns,
still free of the erosion of sorrow. It is pure denial:
I have few excuses, but it's more than I can bear.

Eating with Fingers

I've returned to South Carolina
where summer is barefaced and plain-
   speaking, no dalliance here in Dixie.
For three days, I am comforted
   by the lingering spice of your *daal*
in my fingers, and somehow
   while it lasts, it is enough.
Still I am sure I will return
   without warning to Marlowe's dark
Thames, that ancient stream
   on whose southern banks New World
Kurtzes rave among the natives.
   I will come incognito, travelling light,
and seek out the shelter
   of your sun-washed loft, there
to make poems and scoop
   handsful of *basmati*
souped in your garlic-flecked sauces.

Umpire at the Portrait Gallery

At the Portrait Gallery near Trafalgar Square
I am searched by an ancient umpire
who mumbles his request with marbles or loose
dentures in his mouth. I see my first
portrait: the blotched bony fingers, the warts,
the clumsy overlarge gold ring loosely turning
like it will when he is entombed for good;
that look of boredom around the eyes
he masks with considered politeness
like a drunk man's careful compensations
and this self-important thinning of lips;
the nose, the greenish veins, the cliché
of a mole on his brow. It is too dark here
to study him well, besides he has found nothing
and the natives are restless at my back.

I am looking for the faces of this country;
the rustic, the jaundiced, the worn,
sharp tight snaps so close the pores talk;
faces caught in unaware blankness,
the rituals of rocking to numb silence
on the trains; dirty light, the thin
mist of darkness in the underground
making the faces collectors' bits,
keepables of a post-nuclear tribe.

I find only the posed stateliness
of another time—the courtly manners,

the clean colors staring from the palette
masking the stench and filth of older ways—
nothing to write about, really, nothing.

I am back in the lobby staring at the native,
his Adam's apple bobbing, his fingers,
the thick blackened nails, the stale suit,
the cap, the poem he is—the simple grammar
of another time—the years of the bombs
falling; he must have seen broken bodies
too. Now he fingers my underthings
searching for what I may have taken.
He finds nothing, nods me along.
Still, the globular ring keeps me
from forgetting him altogether,
that and the absence of stories to tell.
It is brilliant outside. A black-faced
Bobby points me the way to the Southern
Bank where the river reeks of history
and word weavers converge in snotty halls
to flaunt their musings to the world.
Here we are in the carcass of empire
searching in vain for sweetest honey.

Reaper in a Wheat Field

in the breeze from an open window
his bones
clatter like music

Toi Derricotte

Wheat lies low. The palette is thick. A butter knife
slashes the paste stinking of turpentine on old canvas.
Only you could live so perfect a sun all your life;
round, finished, no hint that it hid your rotting carcass.

That reaper, they tell me, is death. I see a peasant
pathing his way through annoying dust with his crescent
tool, nothing heroic, just this accessible and mythic thing.
I have never walked among fields of wheat, never seen
a sun so clear in the sky, but I learnt well the genius
of finding death embroidered in your elaborate conceits.

Somewhere on the edge of despair, where it all began:
the plotting, the loading of the weapon, the long walk
into the fields, the sharp crack of the gun, the wound,
the bloody red stumbling through the woods, among the stalks
of gathered wheat; I imagined the reaper as an icon of the dead.

It is late summer in Scotland, the fields stretch yellow
and bare, the sun is a tender ball above a mountain
of biblical clouds. I think of ways to mourn you
as I travel across this island to meet you once more.

Bridge

For Samuel Selvon (1926–1993)

The builder built his bridges with delicate
strips of humor and the stones of love.
Still, what good is a bridge if it obscures
the danger beneath? We used to prance across

ignorant of the turbulence below.
There was a divide we never quite fathomed.
We entered strange villages as if we always belonged
to them—perhaps it was youth, perhaps laughter.

But it is not very funny now.
We woke this morning to see the broken bridge,
its entrails hanging over the river,
pieces of freshly shattered stone plopping

into the sucking water below. The other
village seemed so far away. No one was
laughing. The sky was gray, but what else
could it be on such a morning?

We filed into the chapel to remember,
our eyes still sucked into the vacuum
left between one bank and the other.
We are dying quickly.

Tonight, I stand on the bank and try to laugh,
watching the ribbons of light from my belly
become a maybe bridge. And why not?
Was it not faith that once took us across?

Cortege on Leyton High Road

This morning on Leyton High Road
I watched the too quick cortege
   of glossy black sedans crowned with
plastic encased flowers. And
   for the first time in my life,
I wondered at the incongruity
   of carnations and death.
It is so with London for me:
   death always seems absurdly comic;
Brit wit, I offer; but then
   I am used to the calamity of sirens,
the open shore of mourners,
   the wailing, the stench of duppies in the air,
the litany of blood and spirit
   caught in the sun's rotting heat.

If I die in this sterile city,
no one, I fear, will know the language
   of lamentation, and I will fade simply,
quietly like some nondescript
   bookish cleric barely remembered
by stoic friends at the pub over a pint:
   He was a nice chap, he was;
wrote odd poems, he did,
   so let's have another for him, shall we.
Even the leaves shedding themselves
   will smell more thickly
of death and loss than these mourners.

Memory of a Garden

The dignified mourners, blued
by the waning light, shawled in silk,
transparent as their sorrow, crawl
through the meandering paths of this garden,
while a woman makes flowers grow with the care
of a bent back, a head bandaged in ivory,
the language of her floral pattern,
carmine like wine against the godly
cobalt—it is as if the dappled grace
of the blooms she husbands have infected her skin
with their stippled light and she is nothing
but an apparition in this garden, as the mourners,
in their somber fabrics of mauve and the
bleeding spots of lament, grow pale as death,
eyes as hollow as the rented cave of miracles.

A voice gathers the dusk about them;
no light in the strummed guitar, just the groan
of low chords. It is a song of flower buds turning black
on an April night, branches frosted white like lepers;
of farmers who fret in the glow of yellow bonfires
that flicker between their contorted peach trees
with their miserly warmth against the cold air.
The song is the dull gray of a country's death,
its history caught in this sunfall.
The women continue their dirge-rigid walk
through the plague of flowers while the light
wavers over the bent gardener,
her open palms loam-dark in the gloom.

Excursion to Port Royal

i am inside of
history
its
hungrier than i
thot.

Ishmael Reed

In the giddy house   the wind riots on the beach
where we have had a lunch of flat moist sandwiches cooked
by the steaming bus engine   now alone
abandoned by the other boys   I stare across the roll of sea
there is no sign of the passing of time

no evidence of the decades of progress
only the scraggly grass   the Institute of Jamaica
tourist information plaque screwed tight
into the armory wall   here is the possibility of journey
from the quarterdeck I claim all I survey

on Admiral Nelson's quarterdeck the sea sand is black
shells glint white in the tick of waves
the water is moving   the horizon shifts   the morning's clean edge
smudges into stark sheets of white light   a thin line of cloud
moves   the wind toying with its tail

cannon crusted with centuries of rust black sea sand   dirt points
Admiral Nelson surveys the royal port from his quarterdeck
goblet of gold rum swishing in his unsteady hands   the bitch is singing
from the wooden whorehouse a blue Yorkshire shanty   her tongue
is heavy on the vowels   his dick is erect

here was Napoleon's nemesis too   long-haired bitch with a royal name
teasing the rum to flame in the sweet roast fish air   singing Josephines
their tongues dancing   in the voice you smell their sex
Nelson searches the horizon for ship sail needling its way
across the fabric of green silk looking for war

the shore crunches   laps   folds   unfolds   ticks   gravels
its undertow back out to the seaweed bed   the last of the rum
warms sweetly in his pit   the voice sirens across the quad
and making his giddy way past the armory   combustible
as this itch in his pants   Nelson prays for the empire

III

Art Appreciation

1

There is an Aztec helmet of silver veined with magenta—old blood or
the thin lines of pink like the spewed phlegm of a three-day-old cold.

2

I am a far way from the jungle and the Latin stench of *los conquista-
dores*.

3

A boy chews on a poisonous leaf certain that it is that acidic crisp
leaf he always eats. It is not the leaf he always eats. It is a flowering
shrub, with leaves broad like spinach ears. And he eats, and eats.
Then he vomits, and a thin streak of green slices through the bright
red and bubble of his flaming throat and mouth, a jungle of songs.
He could die but he lives and grows old.

4

The Aztec helmet glimmers in the sodden earth's unnatural vegeta-
tion. Catching the sun after centuries—defying death—it remains
my talisman. Though I cannot read it, I collect its image from glossy
magazines; the silver helmet bursting from soil. I tear out sheets and
sheets, then match them to the decor of my many rooms.

History Cartoon

after a drawing by Kafka

In Prague in 1908
   (the date could be wrong of course
but it was Prague, of this we're sure)
   Jesus stood on a stained bed sheet
the oil lamp's glow
   making a tidy silhouette of him.
The clothesline swayed
   in the smoky air, two metal
stands (crucifixes, really)
   squeaked cartoon-like
planted shallow in gravel and glass.
   And Jesus, bored with it all,
stepped away from the screen
   of projected light.
This was my first miracle,
   another false christ reneging
on the deal he had made.
   The next day someone important
was shot and everyone began
   to fight. The smell of the dead
still rises on damp days
   from the cobblestones
somewhere in Prague,
   of which we are quite certain.

Gothic

This is no cliché, simply
the archetype of who we are,
a nation of mothers.

The daughter holds her bottle.
The mother, the Word.
The son hitches to her side,
his eyes looking off.

There is no cross in the church,
just the black line of the bench
crossed by the splintered stockinged
leg of the mother—there's blood on the floor.

The stoic reserve
of this family is no cliché,
the archetype of who we are,
a nation of mothers.

Marriage

"If I have no offers for big Beulah, she's coming back to you darling"
—*Edna to Norman Manley. London*

Beulah, she, looking at me with her
    tender cat eye, her cheekbones
high, hair cropped low, and I take
    my time to watch her, the way
her left breast is caught between
    her knee and her arm, and
the nipple pulps like a fruit.

Give a man this shaped granite
    stone, and he will run his fingers
over its roughness, imagining the womb
    of his marriage bed, the allegories
of a nation wed to its infant self,
    the allusions to that New Jerusalem
the land of promise, the Blakean hope
    of new mornings. But he sees
the pubescent enigma of a girl
    staring back at the chaos of lust
congealing behind his conqueror's eye.

    You knew this when you made her,
tenderly shaped her, dragged her off
    the hill's path and placed her here
in the sanctity of your home, offering
    her like Sarah would, longing to see
her birth the nation—for she is the queen

of the mountain, the heir-apparent,
the virgin mother of a foetus nation
   wrestling at the portals of its
arrival—you must have known
   he would imagine her tender
on his fingers, softly touching her breast
   while you were not looking.

But I see in this stone song
   a delicate sonnet of lasting grace;
the girl from the hills, too young
   to know that her eyes carry music
and the subtle whisper of lust.
   You give it to your husband
understanding well the strategies
   of love—stone cold, a figment
of his dreams, but close enough
   for comfort and passion.

She is made, your spirit
   in the stone, your music in her eyes
your handwriting in her nude.
   She is the mistress from
the hills, balancing her
   belongings on her head, the Jamaican
dawta he could not marry,
   the earth's skin he could not taste.
You with your bone white hands
   give to him your sacrifice
of love, here in Beulah's land
   while we, the heathens, call it sin.

Hymn

After Olmec Maya Hymn to the Sun IV *by Aubrey William*

The eye is a cotton sheet broken by the web
of crushed wax, dark veins, the crisscross
of tamarind branches against a striped sunset;
at his back, how the birds squeak. He is falling
into a frame of purple tapering into black.
He is retrieving familiar rhythms. His stomach,
in those mornings before light, tastes love or lust,
longing to see her briefly, secretly behind the door barely ajar.

He wants to place a priest with a bloody knife
in the belly of this image. His eyes constantly return
to a woman on the altar, naked, the way her throat jumps,
her eyes dilate in the sun; and it is not long before she is you
coy behind the screen, kissing him with smiles
carved with shadow and yellow softer light.

Grace

The clean lamplight cuts even shadows across the faces.
Grotesquely full faces chew potatoes and swallow black bitter coffee.

The walls, bubbled and uneven, close in on the gathering.
A family sits here against the grate.
It is not hard to see these faces upturned in caskets.

When the potatoes, pried from the hard earth, are gone,
hunger will crawl back into limbs, and the pregnant woman
will feel her child sucking sap from her.

She pours the coffee into quaint demitasses while the gangrene
of the night light stains her skin. This is food for living. Their hands
are black as the earth. Their bodies face new days like winter corpses
poking out from the soil: tenacious sprouts in the hard ground.

The Glory

The candles dance
like poco queen

and the glory
of the Lord

come down

The flames trump
and fall back clean

till the glory
of the Lord

come down

Baptism

1

In a corner of the city
where the seawater meets
the salvaged zinc
of basic shacks, with
their paint pans
packed with soil
she carried from Browns Town
(where everything is luxuriant
but two ends can't meet)
nurturing some cerasee
and mint leaf
trying to turn the beach
into a village
where everything black
even the sand;

you come to play campaigner
on a spirit-filled night
when the earth is rumbling
with the drum and the sub-
terranean journey of spirits
from out the sea bottom
and their heads are lashed
like flags of dignity;

then spinning, spinning
in impossible waves of skirts
white and billowing whiter.

That night at home
you chisel tame the rock
of our salvation in a rush
trying to catch the swirl
before it leaves your head,
trying to contain the knock
of your temple hurling blood
into your arms, your thighs
carving from some ancient
granite the stilled motion
of the dance, the fist
of power, the calm sleep
of wide-eyed possession
the arc of light taking shape
on the body of a believer
and carrier, a mounted
soul, turning, turning,
like it has been doing
since the ships set sail
from the Guinea coast.

2

In 1920 in South Carolina
Africans look like Africans.
They are standing in the river
the lush of swamp vines
thick beards of moss
misting them in soft light.

The girl in the middle with her toes
clutching the mud of the river bottom
is to be dipped back deep, deep
by pastor and deacon full of power
then to be pulled back up
raised above the earth,
wet but the better for it—Amen.

There is a song hanging in the air.
It is morning and a butterfly
turns and flits about
her bandannaed head.

IV

Home Town

I followed you to this characterless place, you call it *home*,
the rough parcels of open acres, a solitary barn in the distance,
and the ubiquitous dwarfed bushes of tobacco.
I have grown accustomed to the flatness of the land, the clean
horizon, and the musty armpitting of our vulnerable bodies.
The sky is bare-faced and incapable of duplicity.

You are weeping because this landscape is a monument
to your miseries—the things you never speak about,
not till now, anyway. There are dead bones in the soil,
you tell me, and these paths, scarring the fertile earth,
sometimes whisper the magic of sorcery at nightfall.
Already the urge to move on. We are failing
at love again, our bodies turned from each other,
and there is stern regret in your eyes when I look.
I feel as if I am being crowded by alien tongues:
what you say to this earth is not easily translated.

In the coolest corner of this restaurant, smelling heavy
of two-day-old collards and a generation of sweat in its walls
we pull at the white flesh of battered fried fish. I carry my mood
like a shield before me, a badge to protect me from the distance of
    language.
We say little, rehearsing the embarrassment of your crying. The bare
landscape outside the window is perfectly balanced, the weight
of an old oak on the right tilting the bland sky upright again.

Parasite

> The silence etched into their skin
> is also mine.
>
> *Yusef Komunyakaa*

I dress in secret, discarding my exile skin.
I constantly pat my pocket to feel the comfort
of my utility accent, exotic as a *slenteng* threnody,
talisman of my alien self, to stand out visible against
the ghostly horde of native sons, their hands slicing the air
in spastic language. I too am disappearing in the mist—a dear price
for feasting on the dead with their thick scent of history.

It is easy in this place to grow comfortable
with the equations that position the land,
the green of tobacco, the scent of magnolia,
the choke-hold, piss-yellow spread of kudzu, so heavy
it bends the chain link fence dividing 277;
the stench of wisteria crawling its pale purple
path through a dying swamp. I hear myself turning
heir to the generation that understood the smell
of burning flesh, the grammar of a stare, the flies
of the dead, undisturbed in an open field. My burden
is far easier, it's true. I have not acquired a taste for chitlins
and grits, but I wear well the livery of ageless anger and quiet
resolve like the chameleon of suffering I am.

Libation

For Ellen

Here is the image of puppies sniffing aspens, garlanded
with rotten leaves so late in winter— Dogwoods, she says.
It's the season of Christ's bleeding, and those dogwoods were planted
as an epitaph to the old actor who howled his lines to empty houses—
before they bore him off on a stage flat, dead.

She tells me of the scarlet ooze of crushed dogwood roots,
this ink used to scratch out poems of lost love on the smooth
white of North Carolina birch. Here in the South
at the bleak end of February I turn bewildered, I find comfort
in the simple affinities of skin, sin, and suffering. I sing tentatively,
knowing too well the warm scent of blood-washed Baptist hymns.

In this fertile loam, new earth to me, the seeds I plant
grow too quickly into sores, septic melons bursting
into startling rot—like overfed guppies.

The dogwood in the wind speckles the bewildered puppies.
I pray among the leaves, pouring libation to thaw the earth.

Tornado Child

For Rosalie Richardson

I am a tornado child.
    I come like a swirl of black and darken up your day;
    I whip it all into my womb, lift you and your things,
    carry you to where you've never been, and maybe,
    if I feel good, I might bring you back, all warm and scared,
    heart humming wild like a bird after early sudden flight.

I am a tornado child.
    I tremble at the elements. When thunder rolls my womb
    trembles, remembering the tweak of contractions
    that tightened to a wail when my mother pushed me out
    into the black of a tornado night.

I am a tornado child,
    you can tell us from far, by the crazy of our hair;
    couldn't tame it if we tried. Even now I tie a bandanna
    to silence the din of anarchy in these coir-thick plaits.

I am a tornado child
    born in the whirl of clouds; the center crumbled,
    then I came. My lovers know the blast of my chaotic giving;
    they tremble at the whip of my supple thighs;
    you cross me at your peril, I swallow light
    when the warm of anger lashes me into a spin,
    the pine trees bend to me swept in my gyrations.

I am a tornado child.
    When the spirit takes my head, I hurtle into the vacuum
    of white sheets billowing and paint a swirl of color,
    streaked with my many songs.

Satta: En Route to Columbia, S.C.

I-Roy rides the gap
where the sax used to rest
and the bass talking
to the Royal man who
can turn a rhyme into sacredness

Want to chant damnation
where my enemies gawk
at the tumbling enjambments
ramming home a truth

Who who who can say
concubine! like tracing
out the wicked's path to hell
like I-Royal, mouth shooting fire?

So, *satta a massa*
says the prophet
cool like a knife edge
and then catch the cross
stick tacking a rhythm
satta a massa gana

I am striding through an alien
landscape, the road smooth
the air heavy with rain
and my heart bluesing along
when the prophet speaks

and it is enough for the grooves
of a forty-five's glimmering vinyl
the comfort of God again on me

Look into the book of life and you will see
that there's a land far far away

Belle

For C.M.T.

Her body is no longer tender, but her mind is free.

Rita Dove

On Devine beside the Tea Room she looks over the moral city,
so old, it has forgotten itself. Her white underpants

of practical cotton are pegged for the sun
and my straying eyes. I have seen her black bras,

startled by their garishness; knowing that she chooses
her wardrobe for this break with tradition, for the neighbors

and silly voyeurs, too afraid to know her when they meet,
who peep for a sign of her flesh in the simplest things,

the scent of her in the flitting fabrics, her laughter
shimmering through the corridors, the texture of her lips

after a sip of iced tea; the dialect of desire in her eyes.
I collect these things, too afraid to speak to her.

Alone now, after leaving him, the farm, and twenty years
of faithful duty, she hangs her things out to dry

defying the neighborly ordinances, the indecency of airing
the collective linen of a people in the unflinching sun.

But in the softer part of night, she feels the absence
of normal things, like a cough, a whisper, someone else's smell,

and she worries about the neighbors, their judgment of her tender
southern belle self. Though she's above pedigree, it's still in the blood,

and she is wracked with that sour guilt of a Baptist sermon
despite her Jewish heart. So in the softer part of the night,

while we sleep, she gathers her exposed things.
Come morning, the balcony is naked as sin.

Hawk

Old Mama talked with her fingers;
sipped her liquor till time stopped.

Old Mama smiled rueful days,
whispered her secrets always

to the faithful wind, always going
some place, coming back forgetful

every time, of whose lips it had kissed,
whose secrets tasted at midnight.

We have lost Mama to the wind,
she left clothes, shoes, pills

and a bag of funky stories behind,
buried in her underthings.

Putting her away, smelling her presence
we break into songs, weaving her sentences

together, like the clumpy plaits she made
of our hair in the soft of kerosene light.

At the graveside, we stare at the swoop
of predator jets, circling the Base,

and Maude walks with Mama's limp,
favoring her right ankle, like Mama did,

muttering 'bout the way it twisted when she ran
from the snort of a white stallion

on that slate gray Carolina dawn
when the cotton fields were blanched,

and the wind was passing by, quiet-quiet,
the diving hawks still screaming.

Sabbath

Early Sunday morning,
there on the bulwark of Fort Sumter,
　where everything turned bloody;
　I stare out to sea and the mist
　blows a ghost ship towards me.
It is all quite normal the way
　I weep in the moment of knowing.
It is the *Amistad*, with Joseph Cinqué
　at the helm, calmly surveying
the folds of the sea, the bloated gulls.
　And a song turns in my head,
edging my teeth with sorrow;
　the salt of long-gone days, the tears.

Wisteria

Circumspect woman,
you carry your memories
tied up in a lipstick-stained
kerchief in a worn straw basket.
When you undo the knot,
the scent of wisteria,
thick with the nausea of nostalgia,
fills the closed-in room.

You lean into the microphone,
smile at the turning tape,
while fingering the fading petals.
You intone your history,
breathing in the muggy
scent of wayward love.
Your anger is always
a whisper, enigmatic,
almost unspoken,
just a steady heat.

I don't like 'em
never did, never could . . .

Midland

For Krystal

I

A Letter From Greeleyville

Dear Claudia,
Few things here succumb to time though the old grow tender
and die. Still, they appear again in the new light,
same face, same open skirts, same fingers clutching pipes
smoking a halo about their heads, rocking a blues on the same porches.
You would like this place for a time, but I know you will long
for the clean efficiency of your city—the stench of manufactured age.
The scent of jasmine and the dank earthiness of this soil
soaked by an old river, so long silted by the runoff
of a generation of fears, detritus, and funky bundles
of hair, sin, phlegm, blood passed out each month,
shoved, clumped, burnt into the blooming ground, remind me
of Sturge Town in St. Ann where my grandfather is buried
in a thick grotto of *aloe vera* and stunted pimiento trees.
But this place speaks a language I have to learn, and this woman
who travels with me introduces me to the earth and her folks
as a stranger, a specimen from a far way. I pretend I do not feel
the welling of tears when I smell the old sweat of her grandmother's
housedress hanging from a nail on the back of an oak door.
The corn has turned a rotten gold and pale in the summer,
the twine of leaves and roots dark and spotted while the mildewed glory
of old hymnals seeps from the St. James Baptist church

where the blues have marinated the boards till they are supple
with the fluent pliability of faith so old it knows the ways of God
like it knows family, and blood ties. I am stealing things from here
and sending them to you, knowing you are too decent to use them.
But do, keep them safe till I arrive for a spell, and then I will find
good use for these sweet collectibles, lasting things. Love, Kwame.

II

Blues on Highway Fifteen with Krystal

At midmorning, we watch the green of tobacco stanzas,
such even reckoning of this state where a nation carved its name
into Cherokee country, making a new landscape, plows turning the earth
to the slow assured cadence of the Baptist hymns, the rebel yells,
the scalper's knife. Yet there is something tender here.

We are riding Highway Fifteen through Manning toward Kingstree,
searching for Alma's meditation on home in the sweetly pained
bourbon-grooved voice of Lady Day that Krystal plays
again and again, punching viciously at the knobs, rushing the tape
back to its beginning. And Lady Day conjures the skeletal twist of an oak
somewhere where the torture of fear and the faraway cry of the dead
are the same, despite the tundra cold. Krystal points to a green bluff,
a tree isolated against an indifferent blue sky—*Like that,* she says.
*The common trees, the quality of light in the sky. I sat under that tree
once—I don't remember why, but we sat there, me and my mother,
and we ate sandwiches, and she was crying for no good reason.*

III

In Search of Alma

After the storm, the ravaging of the earth,
the stripping of green, the pounding of winds
on tender flesh; after the howling,
the green grows hungrily over everything,
and how quickly the multitude of sins
is covered by the crawling of wisteria and kudzu.
This earth speaks no memories of wrongs done;
there is a sweet politeness here, a way of decency,
the value of perfume in damp kerchiefs outside
the outhouse where the flies buzz rudely.

I have come to seek out Alma's lament,
to scratch into her grave, and find the rot,
of crumbling softness that was her paler self.

IV

Crow over Corn Row

Above the shock of cotton trees hangs a solitary
bird, against the sky. It is black and stays only long enough
to seem like a portent. Standing in the cotton groves, I pluck
the coarse filthy white tangle from the gray brittle unlipping
of the flower. There is nothing like the hint of a vulva's softness here;
all juice dried out, the earth gives up its beaten self
in the language of simple cotton, the tight tangle
of the squat bushes, the debris from years of shedding
upturned like the unexpected shallow graves
of massacred millions. I pluck at the stubborn seeds
until the ball of cotton is softer in my palm.
The bird swoops, turns, and fades into the blue.
This short peace defies the rustle of old ghosts
quarreling in the twisted ribbons of the corn leaves.
It is hard to breathe in this heat and stench; easier to drive on,
the wind cupped by the car, warm relief on a wet body.

V

Roosting

I drive toward the burnt-out Baptist church
with its well-kept graveyard — green, flowered —
and blackened walls desecrated with familiar
hatred, hieroglyphs of a twisted myth.

"You have just received a courtesy call from the knights
of the Ku Klux Klan. Don't make the next be a business call."

I remember the bird, black as a crow
or raven chattering over the cacophony of corn,
uncertain of a place to land, so he moved on.

But the symbol is too convenient — too balanced.

Now a flock of audacious crows stare
into the gutted sanctuary, shaded by the fresh
whiteness of blooming dogwood.
They are roosting, as if they have found a place to haunt,
as if the feet of some long forgotten dead
were shod with shoes for walking by ignorant folks,
as if no one pointed their heads East to home.

I keep a piece of burnt timber as a souvenir,
my fingers growing black with the soot.
The silence prays over me.

VI

Decent Folk

A voice, high as a countertenor, shatters the eaves;
the aria of a storm twists its path through
the thick peach groves of this blood-soaked land
high like a castrato gallivanting through
a Handel requiem, a lament for the dead;
this sound is bearded, broad-chested and cynical,
it is ripping through the state, now, seasoned
by the warmth of Florida's serrated coastline,
and the family gathers to whisper prayers as the world
crumbles around them. The blackness is heavy.
They pass down their stories to the wail of death
warding off the tears with the preserved narratives
of survival. What they speak are lies, the truths
are entombed secrets, the ritual secrets of rural folk,
still decent enough to know that talking about
love between that cracker Buddy Lawrence
and Powie, sweet Powie, is sacrilege, sinful,
plain indecent. No one thinks to ask how
twelve babies, yellow and pink, came howling
from that smoky womb. No one thinks to ask
how come he dies there in the house he built
for her, the wind blowing like it is now,
and the next generation staring at this man,
this white man breathing his last right under
the flared nostrils of Jimmy Crow. No one asks
nothing. Powie was raped, is all. The rest
is silence and the dignity of black folks

cultivated on this equivocal land, the rows
even, the time of harvest arriving like the moon,
relentless, the way it has always been, always will be.

VII

Epoch

> "I moan this way 'cause he's dead," she said.
> "Then tell me, who is that laughing upstairs?"
> "Them's my sons. They glad."
>
> Invisible Man *by Ralph Ellison*

Krystal, an epoch glows beneath your skin.
Your nose spreads like flattened clay, your lips,
bloody grapefruit, wet, startled crimson.
You hurried your makeup, and the base is too pale
for your skin. You have no time for the paletting,
the mixing of hues to find the dialect of your history.
There is the epoch of silence in your skin,
something hidden, a curse in the long of your lower back
before the deviance of your buttocks.
A family of tangerine people; your folk are black,
thoroughly African, southern folk shaped in the kerosene-smelling
back quarters, where old pork was cured; at night, the flies, groggy,
drunk with the heat, and Buddy Lawrence panting into this soil,
this tendon tight woman, making babies with transparent skin.
Powie begat Alma begat Okla begat Lynne begat Krystal: the years
do not seem enough between the ash and tar of a Sumter lynching
and the promise of better days. Your skin does not trust its language
of appeasement. You stand in the stark sun, trying to darken your skin,
but it grows transparent in the heat, and all is palimpsest,
the language of blood underneath your skin.

VIII

To the Third and Fourth Generations

You too carry the soup of nausea, the taste of a man's forced breath
behind you, the crawl of his hands cupping at your flesh,
the thought of dreaming your face into the wide spaces of the low country
where the bandy-legged, tobacco chewing cliché of a farmer came to find
the perfect lip and tongue of your ancestor. Still, at night,
you dream his head, too heavy for the smallness of his body,
his tiny hands open, trying to touch your nipple.
And you wish for an instant that he were the cracker, Buddy Lawrence,
so you could, for Powie, for Alma, for the host of mothers, leave him
    castrated
and bleeding in the half light. But his hair kinks, his eyes are black
as Elmina's dungeons, and his smile reeks of the disarming sweet of a
    Motown song.
You will not write this down. You will store it quietly, like Powie did,
trusting that the ruined cells will seed in another womb, another
    generation
free enough to speak the genetic vernacular of anger.

IX

Somebody Trouble the Water

Wade in the water
Wade in the water, children
Wade in the water . . .

In a dream, I am in the Sahara with its tongue of heat
on the edges of Egypt. The sand is carnelian, stained with old sacrificial
    pots.
The shards are all that remain. It has been centuries and still,
in the early morning, a girl walks slowly, the soft sand slipping under her
    feet;
a smudge of white flutters in her hands rippled by the wind's lick.
On a perfectly smooth rock, she batters the tender dove,
its blood gleaming on the stone. She pulls out the soft viscera
and reads them while the new sun splatters the mountain's face.
She is a dream so distant she seems worth forgetting.
But she changes, as dreams tend to, and it is you, Krystal, who stands
    there,
over the grave of Alma, this time, your palms open, the wet tissue speckled
by the green above you. You have been crying, making, I can tell,
unreasonable covenants with the dead, with the living,
with the mountains at your back in this place of silence.
This South's sores are still too fresh. A hand plunged
into the earth will touch the sticky moisture of its brokenness.
You've got to sing those songs just to keep on keeping on, Krystal.

Wade in the water
Wade in the water, children

86

Wade in the water
God's gonna trouble the water
God's gonna trouble the water.

Love Oil

For Lana

1

I saw how they trimmed you down,
called you Rosie, like a pet dog,
and you smiled and called the boy
same age as me, Mister, like you calling

love. How you grabbed him up from the grass
when fire ants took at us in the yard,
and you made your face like it was
your own feet aflame with sting;

you bawled me down for being such a fool
for not knowing no better than to take the boy
out into the yard like that, telling me
to go get my legs all washed off

stead of standing there with my eyes all wet
like a fool or something worse.
Saw how you laid him down
and sung your song oiling your palms

soothing him like a baby
his eyes drinking you in.

2

You complain of the arthritis in your legs
when the rain gathers over the swamp
and I drive through the fog to find you
and fill my hands with sharp Bengay

and I love those legs, mother, love
those veins, green on your tender yellow skin,
with songs you never sang for me, Mama,
with tender I ever felt for you.

Easter Sunday

"I was getting savage."

Joseph Conrad

The nail clip unfolded, catches the light
like an origami insect of aluminum foil.
My nails, crudely clipped, gather in a pile
of opaque ivory on the gleaming porcelain,
waiting among the single pubic hair
like the paraphernalia of an obeah man
about to tie me for good. I can
stare at these meaningless objects
of my life, the evidence of flesh remaking
itself, the rituals of the civilized,
warding off the encroachment of the beast,
the barren heart of a callous ape.
I read *National Geographic*s on the toilet
after midnight, to calm my dreams
now taking shape around the sound
Rosewood, the brute film of Florida's
lynching history; so familiar the cowardly
bravado of white men spewing *nigger*
like an aphrodisiac for their impotent selves.
I do not want to dream of blood tonight;
tomorrow is purple resurrection day, Christ's
ginal game, that genius disappearance.
I want to break unleavened bread
with my brother, son of the beast in the dark
grinning at the charred stump of a black man
turning in the kerosene haze of Rosewood.

I clip my nails, watch the projectile crescents
dart around the tile until I am man again,
trimmed to the clawless perfection of man.
Now, perhaps, I will dream of fossils,
the primordial sway of a Yanomami hammock,
and the bland narratives of alien people,
Von Humboldt's "fierce people" guarding the portals
of the Orinoco's source. I transfer my dialect of ire
into myth; trying to beat back that lament
of a gospel song, blue and relentless as truth,
unfolding the apostrophe of the hung man dangling
from a live oak like the worm's silk cocoon.

Notes

"Two Premonitions"—For SS
"Sanctuary"—After *Starry Night* by Vincent Van Gogh
"Sun Strokes"—After *Sunspot Maximum* by Aubrey Williams
"Baptism"—After *Jamaican Gothic* (1968) by Karl Parboosingh
"Grace"—After *Potato Eaters* by Vincent Van Gogh

Thanks to Sarah Maguire, Claudia Rankine, Sudeep Sen, Melissa Johnson, Colin Channer, Larry Lieberman, Olive Senior, Dionne Brand, Shara McCallum, Susan Ludvigson, Mervyn Morris, Lucia Getsi, Ed Madden and Ellen Arl for looking at these poems and telling me what to do with them.

Thanks also to the Department of English, University of South Carolina for space and time to write. Thanks to the South Sumter Resource Center and Lana Odom for giving me stories to tell and for teaching me the dialect of home. Thanks to Krystal Kenely for her family's stories and for the dignity and grace of Midland folk.

DATE DUE